MW00897380

Animal Songs

Illustrated by Pat Magers

Random House 🏠 New York

The Animal Song

Alligator, hedgehog, anteater, bear,
Rattlesnake, buffalo, anaconda, hare;
Bullfrog, woodchuck, wolverine, goose,
Whippoorwill, chipmunk, jackal, moose.

Ha, ha, ha, hee, hee, hee,
How many animals do you see?

Ha, ha, ha, ho, ho, ho,
How many animals do you know?

Mud turtle, whale, glowworm, bat,
Salamander, snail, and Maltese cat;
Polecat, dog, wild otter, rat,
Pelican, hog, dodo, and bat.

Ha, ha, ha, hee, hee, hee,
How many animals do you see?

Ha, ha, ha, ho, ho, ho,
How many animals do you know?

Oh Where, Oh Where Has My Little Dog Gone?

Oh where, oh where has my little dog gone?
Oh where, oh where can he be?
With his ears cut short and his tail cut long,
Oh where, oh where can he be?

Pop! Goes the Weasel

All around the cobbler's bench,
The monkey chased the weasel;
The monkey thought 'twas all in fun,
Pop! goes the weasel.

A penny for a spool of thread,
A penny for a needle;
That's the way the money goes,
Pop! goes the weasel.

Three Little Kittens

Three little kittens, they lost their mittens,
And they began to cry:
"Oh, Mother dear, see here, see here,
Our mittens we have lost!"
"What, lost your mittens? You naughty kittens!
Then you shall have no pie."
"Meow! Meow! Meow! Meow! Meow! Meow! Meow!"

Three little kittens, they found their mittens,
And they began to cry:
"Oh, Mother dear, see here, see here,
Our mittens we have found!"
"What, found your mittens? You darling kittens!
Then you shall have some pie."
"Meow! Meow! Meow! Meow! Meow! Meow! Meow!"

Cluck-Cluck! (The Chicken Song)

Cluck-cluck! Cluck-cluck-cluck!
Good morning, Mrs. Hen.
How many chickens have you got?
Madam, I've got ten.
Four of them are yellow,
And four of them are brown,
And two of them are speckled red,
The nicest in the town.

Six Little Ducks

Six little ducks that I once knew,
Fat ones, skinny ones, they were too;
But the one little duck with the feather on his back,
He led the others with his "Quack quack quack! Quack quack quack!"
He led the others with his "Quack quack quack!"

Down to the water they would go,
Wibble-wobble, wibble-wobble, to and fro;
But the one little duck with the feather on his back,
He led the others with his "Quack quack quack! Quack quack quack!"
He led the others with his "Quack quack quack!"

Home from the water they would come,
Wibble-wobble, wibble-wobble, ho ho hum!
But the one little duck with the feather on his back,
He led the others with his "Quack quack quack! Quack quack quack!"
He led the others with his "Quack quack quack!"

The Farmer in the Dell

The farmer in the dell,
The farmer in the dell,
Heigh ho! the derry-o!
The farmer in the dell.

The farmer takes a wife,
The farmer takes a wife,
Heigh ho! the derry-o!
The farmer takes a wife.

The wife takes a child,
The wife takes a child,
Heigh ho! the derry-o!
The wife takes a child.

The child takes a nurse,
The child takes a nurse,
Heigh ho! the derry-o!
The child takes a nurse.

The nurse takes a dog,
The nurse takes a dog,
Heigh ho! the derry-o!
The nurse takes a dog.

The dog takes a cat,
The dog takes a cat,
Heigh ho! the derry-o!
The dog takes a cat.

The cat takes a rat,
The cat takes a rat,
Heigh ho! the derry-o!
The cat takes a rat.

The rat takes the cheese,
The rat takes the cheese,
Heigh ho! the derry-o!
The rat takes the cheese.

The cheese stands alone,
The cheese stands alone,
Heigh ho! the derry-o!
The cheese stands alone.

The Bear Went Over the Mountain

The bear went over the mountain,
The bear went over the mountain,
The bear went over the mountain
To see what he could see.

To see what he could see,
To see what he could see,
The bear went over the mountain
To see what he could see.

The other side of the mountain,
The other side of the mountain,
The other side of the mountain
Was all that he could see.

Was all that he could see,
Was all that he could see,
The other side of the mountain
Was all that he could see.

The Animal Fair

I went to the animal fair,
The birds and the beasts were there;
The big baboon by the light of the moon
Was combing his auburn hair.

You ought to have seen the monk,
He jumped on the elephant's trunk;
The elephant sneezed and fell on his knees,
And what became of the monk, the monk?
And what became of the monk?

Froggie Went A-Courtin'

Froggie went a-courtin', he did ride.
H'm, h'm, h'm, h'm.
Froggie went a-courtin', he did ride,
With a sword and a pistol by his side.
H'm, h'm, h'm, h'm.

He rode up to Miss Mousie's den.
H'm, h'm, h'm, h'm.
He rode up to Miss Mousie's den,
Said, "Please, Miss Mousie, won't you let me in?"
H'm, h'm, h'm, h'm.

"Yes, Sir Frog, I sit and spin."
H'm, h'm, h'm, h'm.
"Yes, Sir Frog, I sit and spin;
Pray, Mister Froggie, won't you walk in?"
H'm, h'm, h'm, h'm.

The frog said, "My dear, I've come to see."
H'm, h'm, h'm, h'm.
The frog said, "My dear, I've come to see
If you, Miss Mousie, will marry me."
H'm, h'm, h'm, h'm.

"I don't know what to say to that."
H'm, h'm, h'm, h'm.
"I don't know what to say to that
Till I speak with my uncle Rat."
H'm, h'm, h'm, h'm.

When Uncle Rat came riding home,
H'm, h'm, h'm, h'm.
When Uncle Rat came riding home,
Said he, "Who's been here since I've been gone?"
H'm, h'm, h'm, h'm.

"A fine young froggie has been here."
H'm, h'm, h'm, h'm.
"A fine young froggie has been here;
He means to marry me, it's clear."
H'm, h'm, h'm, h'm.

So Uncle Rat, he rode to town.
H'm, h'm, h'm, h'm.
So Uncle Rat, he rode to town
And bought his niece a wedding gown.
H'm, h'm, h'm, h'm.

The frog and the mouse, they went to France.
H'm, h'm, h'm, h'm.
The frog and the mouse, they went to France,
And that's the end of my romance.
H'm, h'm, h'm, h'm.

Over in the Meadow

Over in the meadow, in the sand, in the sun,
Lived an old mother frog and her little froggie one.
"Croak!" said the mother. "I croak," said the one.
So they croaked and they croaked in the sand, in the sun.

Over in the meadow, in the stream so blue,
Lived an old mother fish and her little fishies two.
"Swim!" said the mother. "We swim," said the two.
So they swam and they swam in the stream so blue.

Over in the meadow, on a branch of the tree,
Lived an old mother bird and her little birdies three.
"Sing!" said the mother. "We sing," said the three.
So they sang and they sang on a branch of the tree.

The Fox

The fox went out in the chilly night;
He prayed for the moon to give him light.
He'd many a mile to go that night
Before he reached the town-o, town-o, town-o.
He'd many a mile to go that night
Before he reached the town-o.

He ran till he came to a great big bin;
The ducks and the geese were kept therein.
"A couple of you will grease my chin
Before I leave this town-o, town-o, town-o.
A couple of you will grease my chin
Before I leave this town-o."

He grabbed a gray goose by the neck
And threw a duck across his back.
He didn't mind their quack, quack, quack
And their legs all dangling down-o, down-o, down-o.
He didn't mind their quack, quack, quack
And their legs all dangling down-o.

Then old Mother Flipper-Flopper jumped out of bed,
And out of the window she stuck her head.
Said, "Get up, John, the gray goose is gone,
And the fox is in the town-o, town-o, town-o."
Said, "Get up, John, the gray goose is gone,
And the fox is in the town-o."

So John, he ran to the top of the hill,
And he blew his horn both loud and shrill.
The fox, he said, "I better flee with my kill,
Or they'll soon be on my trail-o, trail-o, trail-o."
The fox, he said, "I better flee with my kill,
Or they'll soon be on my trail-o."

He ran till he came to his cozy den,
And there were his little ones, eight, nine, ten.
They said, "Daddy, you better go back again,
'Cause it must be a mighty fine town-o, town-o, town-o."
They said, "Daddy, you better go back again,
'Cause it must be a mighty fine town-o."

Little Robin Redbreast

Little Robin Redbreast
Sat upon a tree,
Up went Pussycat
And down went he;
Down came Pussycat,
Away Robin ran,
Said little Robin Redbreast,
"Catch me if you can."

Little Robin Redbreast
Jumped upon a spade,
Pussycat jumped after him
And then he was afraid;
Little Robin chirped and sang,
And what did Pussy say?
Pussycat said, "Mew, mew, mew,"
And Robin flew away.

I Love Little Pussy

I love little pussy,
Her coat is so warm,
And if I don't hurt her,
She'll do me no harm.

I'll sit by the fire
And give her some food,
And pussy will love me
Because I am good.

I love little pussy,
Her coat is so warm,
And if I don't hurt her,
She'll do me no harm.

I'll not pull her tail
Nor drive her away,
Little pussy and I
Very gently will play.

Old MacDonald Had a Farm

Old MacDonald had a farm, E-I-E-I-O!
And on this farm he had a dog, E-I-E-I-O!
With a bow-wow here, and a bow-wow there,
Here a bow, there a bow, everywhere a bow-wow.
Old MacDonald had a farm, E-I-E-I-O!

Old MacDonald had a farm, E-I-E-I-O!
And on this farm he had a cow, E-I-E-I-O!
With a moo-moo here, and a moo-moo there,
Here a moo, there a moo, everywhere a moo-moo,
A bow-wow here, and a bow-wow there,
Here a bow, there a bow, everywhere a bow-wow.
Old MacDonald had a farm, E-I-E-I-O!

Old MacDonald had a farm, E-I-E-I-O!
And on this farm he had a pig, E-I-E-I-O!
With an oink-oink here, and an oink-oink there,
Here an oink, there an oink, everywhere an oink-oink,
A moo-moo here, and a moo-moo there,
Here a moo, there a moo, everywhere a moo-moo,
A bow-wow here, and a bow-wow there,
Here a bow, there a bow, everywhere a bow-wow.
Old MacDonald had a farm, E-I-E-I-O!

Old MacDonald had a farm, E-I-E-I-O!
And on this farm he had a horse, E-I-E-I-O!
With a neigh-neigh here, and a neigh-neigh there,
Here a neigh, there a neigh, everywhere a neigh-neigh,
An oink-oink here, and an oink-oink there,
Here an oink, there an oink, everywhere an oink-oink,
A moo-moo here, and a moo-moo there,
Here a moo, there a moo, everywhere a moo-moo,
A bow-wow here, and a bow-wow there,
Here a bow, there a bow, everywhere a bow-wow.
Old MacDonald had a farm, E-I-E-I-O!

Fiddle-De-Dee

Fiddle-de-dee, fiddle-de-dee,
The fly has married the bumblebee.
Says the fly, says he,"Will you marry me
And live with me, sweet bumblebee?"
Fiddle-de-dee, fiddle-de-dee,
The fly has married the bumblebee.

Fiddle-de-dee, fiddle-de-dee,
The fly has married the bumblebee.
Says the bee, says she, "I'll live under your wing
And you'll never know I carry a sting."
Fiddle-de-dee, fiddle-de-dee,
The fly has married the bumblebee.

Mary Had a Little Lamb

Mary had a little lamb,
Little lamb, little lamb,
Mary had a little lamb,
Its fleece was white as snow.

And everywhere that Mary went,
Mary went, Mary went,
Everywhere that Mary went,
The lamb was sure to go.

It followed her to school one day,
School one day, school one day,
It followed her to school one day,
Which was against the rule.

It made the children laugh and play,
Laugh and play, laugh and play,
It made the children laugh and play
To see a lamb at school.

Be Kind to Your Webfooted Friends

Be kind to your webfooted friends,
For a duck may be somebody's mother.
They live in the marshes and the swamp,
Where the weather is cold and damp.

You may think that this is the end.
Well, it isn't, for there is another chorus.

Be kind to your webfooted friends,
For a duck may be somebody's mother.
They live in the marshes and the swamp,
Where the weather is cold and damp.

You may think that this is the end.
Well, it is!